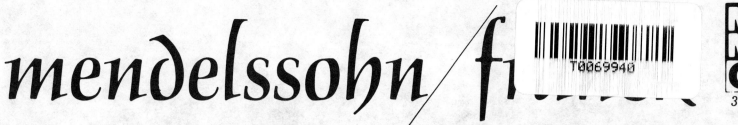

mendelssohn/franck

CAPRICCIO BRILLANT, OP. 22 FOR PIANO AND ORCHESTRA (ORCHESTRAL ACCOMPANIMENT) | SYMPHONIC VARIATIONS FOR PIANO AND ORCHESTRA (ORCHESTRAL ACCOMPANIMENT)

MUSIC MINUS ONE PIANO

THE STUTTGART SYMPHONY ORCHESTRA, WILLIAM HARRISON. CONDUCTOR

MMO
327

T0069940

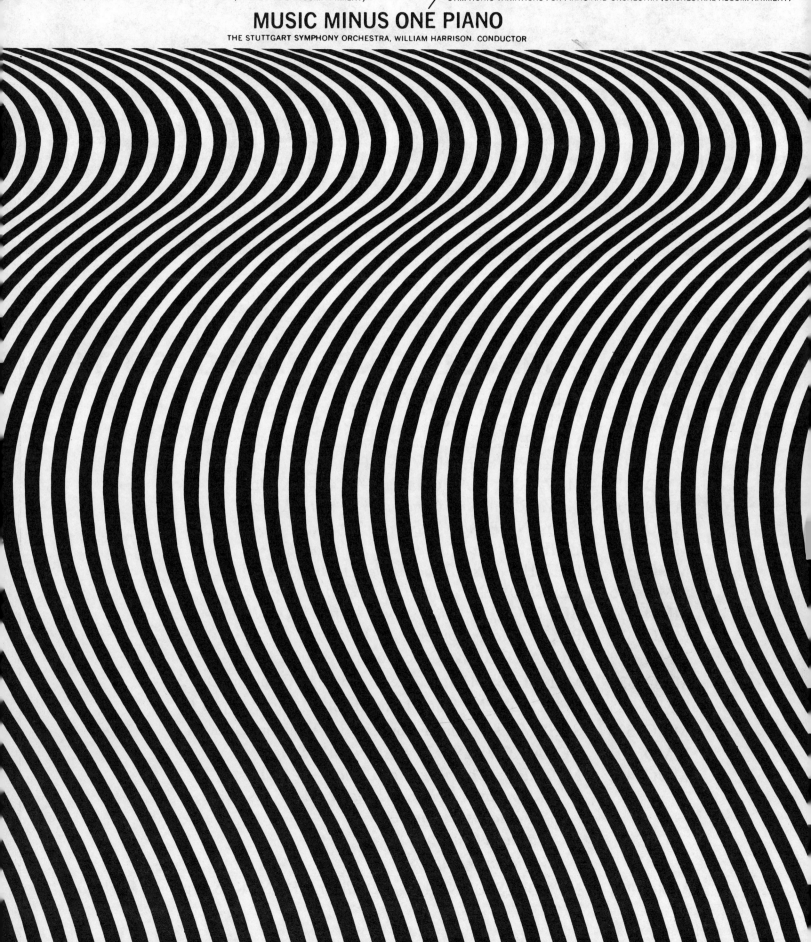

MUSIC MINUS ONE PIANO EDITIONS

felix mendelssohn
Capriccio brillant

6

4 taps precede music to set tempo.

Allegro con fuoco.

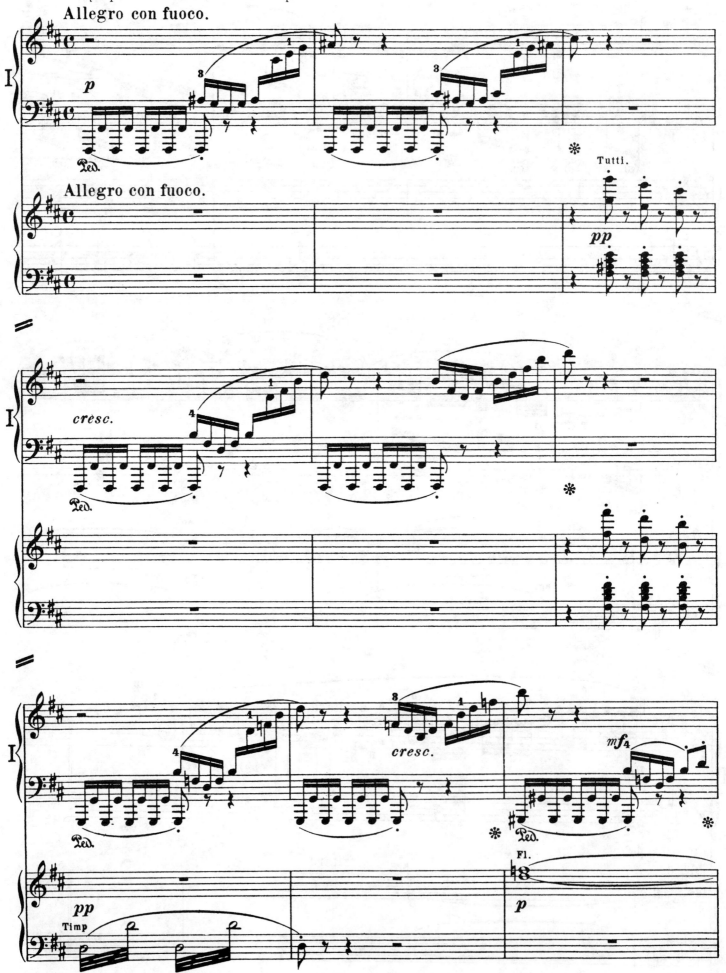

Allegro con fuoco.

cesar franck
symphonic variations
for piano and orchestra

58

2 taps per measure   2 taps per measure   2 taps per measure

Tempo I.

Tempo I.

Br. Vcl.

THINK CASSETTES!!!

In the past few years, the fidelity and pitch perfection of modern cassette machines has improved tremendously. We feel that the necessary quality needed for Music Minus One play-along tapes has now been reached, and have begun to offer all MMO titles in cassette form.

The cassettes are manufactured at one-to-one speeds on premium oxide tapes, and each is mounted on the face of an lp-sized jacket with the music booklet enclosed. Since their introduction in 1983, they have met with enthusiastic acceptance from our clientele. The sound to be heard is equivalent to the original master tapes and is truly *state-of-the-art*.

Our ability to fulfill orders in this exciting new format is 100%! We urge you to think cassettes when ordering. You'll like them in this fine sounding medium and we will be able to service your needs with greater speed and efficiency.

Since the starting point for each selection on this tape will vary according to the particular cassette player being used, may we suggest that you take a moment now and fill in the correct selection positions for your tape, as indicated by your own cassette machine.

This will help you locate each piece when coming back to the tape for repeated use.

SIDE A			SIDE B		
Selection Title		Tape Counter No.	Selection Title		Tape Counter No.
1			1		
2			2		
3			3		
4			4		
5			5		
6			6		
7			7		
8			8		
9			9		
10			10		

Music Minus One uses the finest cassette tape and housings available. However, since we use pre-loaded tape in making our real-time, one-to-one copies, the length of the tape may vary slightly from the length of the music. We suggest that you fast-forward the end of the side before turning the cassette over, from side A to side B.

MUSIC MINUS ONE 50 S. Buckhout St. Irvington, N.Y. 10533